PLAYING TOGETHER
LEARNING TOGETHER

By
JOAN BARRETT
LINDA THOMPSON

Illustrated By
KIMBLE MEAD

GoodYearBooks

An Imprint of ScottForesman
A Division of HarperCollins*Publishers*

GoodYearBooks

are available for most basic curriculum subjects plus many enrichment areas. For more GoodYearBooks, contact your local bookseller or educational dealer. For a complete catalog with information about GoodYearBooks, please write:

GoodYearBooks
ScottForesman
1900 East Lake Avenue
Glenview, Il 60025

Book design by Street Level Studio.
Copyright © 1996 Joan Barrett and Linda Thompson.
All Rights Reserved.
Printed in the United States of America.

ISBN 0-673-36160-8

2 3 4 5 6 7 8 9 - MH - 03 02 01 00 99 98 97 96

Dedication

This book is dedicated to our husbands, John and Bob, both of whom had faith in the concept of this book. Their counsel, patience, and encouragement helped move the book into high gear whenever it began to sputter.

Acknowledgements

A book of this nature needs the cooperation of many people. For their original musical contributions, we thank Mary Murphy and Patti and Michael Roe. For his technical advice on the musical scores, we are indebted to Reverend Charles Faso, OFM, Pastor of St. Peter's Church, Chicago, Illinois. We thank Denise Tady for permission to use her recipe for the Texas Cowboy Bubbles. Also, we are grateful to Robin M. Parsons and Linda A. Bergonia of The Young Cooks Series for permission to reprint their recipe for "No-Cook Fresh Tomato Sauce with Paste". For their good-natured willingness to cooperate with our endeavors, we wish to applaud: Jean, Steve, Stephanie, Geof, Dan, and Ryan Graham; Rita, Mike, John and Bill Higgins; Joe Barrett; Bob, Linda, Meghan, Collin, and Sean Barrett; Mary, David, Caroline Elizabeth, and David J. Murphy; Ed, Kelly, Katie, Jimmy, and Maggie Barrett; and Patti, Mike, Brendan, and Caitrin Roe.

Finally and most importantly, we pay tribute to our publisher, GoodYearBooks of Scott Foresman and their editors, Mario Campanaro, Thomas Nieman, Eden Sommerville and Roberta Dempsey. Because of their confidence in our ability, their professional input, and their unending patience, this book is now a reality.

Table of Contents

JOINT VENTURE

BIBLIOGRAPHY

INTRODUCTION

Play is the work of childhood. It is as important to a child as a job or a career is to an adult. Almost everything that a child does is play. Through this medium a child becomes aware of herself as an individual and aware of her relationship to others and the world. To accomplish this, the book presents a range of activities for you and your child to do together. The emphasis of this book is on the "play" aspect of learning. Learning can and should be fun. Life is fun if approached in the proper way. The overall goal of this book is to encourage better communication between you and your child, forming a special bond that will become stronger as your child grows. Along with this bonding, your child will develop a feeling of self-worth, which is a basic ingredient in the complex process of "learning to learn."

At little or no cost to you, these activities can help your child to progress academically, and teach her to think, to focus on a given task, and to respond to visual and auditory stimuli. They can also help the two of you communicate and bond. As your child progresses through school, making "good" grades may be important to both of you, but remember, one of the most important factors in a child's development is self-esteem. No matter what grades a child achieves, if she feels worthwhile to you and to herself, she will be a much happier person.

Show your pleasure in her success. Children can sense if you are pleased; hug your child often and express your love. She can tell by your eyes and your expressions, the tone of your voice, and your actions that you care and are interested in her. Let her know she is special for herself alone—not for what she can or cannot do. It shouldn't hurt to be a child; it should be a time of joy and laughter and love shared with you—such memories will last both of you a lifetime.

COMMUNICATION

Communicating with your child is the first and most important step in creating a caring relationship between the two of you. Frequent conversations with your child will teach valuable listening skills, encouraging her to focus on words and facial expressions. Soon the child learns that certain sounds and expressions have meaning and importance. A child's ability to think and express logical ideas in everyday conversation allows her to integrate successfully into a world of diverse values and beliefs.

What you say and how you say it are important elements of good communication. It is easy to substitute command-giving for communication: "Don't touch that," "Hang up your clothes," or "Just go watch TV." Instead, discuss the child's feelings about people, places, and everyday events. Your child's concerns might at first appear trivial, but to a child's eyes, small problems often loom large. For your child to become aware that you respect her opinion, even if it may be contrary to your own, helps her realize that you care about her and value her as a person. The very fact that she wishes to share her ideas with you is a goal you should be proud to achieve in your relationship with her.

To start communicating, read stories, poems, and fairy tales to your child. Talk about them after you've read them. Ask questions about the character she liked best, where and when the story took place, how the story made her feel, and so on. Discuss the stories you have read together while you go for walks or do other activities to help her with her recall. Taking an interest in what you have read together will also reinforce her enjoyment of reading. Not only should you read to your child, but she should see you read and enjoy a good book or magazine. Children learn by imitation.

Another way to create a relaxed relationship is to look at family pictures together. Children love to look at familiar pictures, especially pictures of themselves with other members of the family. Show your child several pictures. Talk about the pictures together. If possible, find a variety of pictures—grandma and grandpa when they were little, aunts and uncles and cousins, brothers and sisters, and so on. Explain your relationship and your child's relationship to the people in the pictures.

Do not overwhelm your child with too much family history at once. She will refer back to the family albums through the years. For now center your discussion around the very familiar individuals in her life. Tell stories about your childhood. Explain that you had likes and dislikes, fears and anxieties, the same as she has. Look at pictures of friends. Show her that "family" also includes friends. Even pets make up a family. We're all connected under the broad term "family."

As your child gets older and more aware of the world around her, she will want to talk more about her family and relationships. Be honest. Don't sugarcoat your stories. Establish a sense of trust between you and your child. Tell the truth without being maudlin: "Aunt Sue died when she was quite young." Your child will lead the conversation with questions. When her interest wanes, put your pictures away for another time. This is a very basic way to begin communicating with your child. It shows her that you are human like she is, that you were a child the same as she is. She'll be pleasantly surprised.

Parenting is no easy task. No one has all the answers. But if there were one recipe to follow, its ingredients would include compassion and understanding, nurtured by an open expression of love and trust. Being able to understand and relate to your child when she is young will allow you to appreciate her needs as she grows through the very difficult and confusing stage of adolescence.

Start today. Talk with your child no matter what her age. It can mark the beginning of a new and improved relationship for the two of you. If you are a little uneasy at first, and don't know how to start communicating with your child, the activities in this book will be beneficial to you. You will see that just getting started is the hardest part. Soon you'll be laughing and hugging each other and having a wonderful time.

LEARNING TO LISTEN

Auditory perception is the ability to derive meaning from verbally presented material, or in other words, the ability to listen carefully to the words being spoken and to understand their meaning. To derive meaning from verbally presented material, one must listen to the spoken word. One must be able to focus one's attention on what is being said and at the same time ignore surrounding distractions and noises. The act of listening is a learned ability. Listening is not the same as hearing; it is an activity with a focus and a goal. Listening is necessary for academic achievement. We all must listen to learn. Unless a child listens to the instructions, directions, and information presented in his classroom, his academic achievement is doomed. If he "tunes out" the spoken word, knowledge can hardly be "tuned into" his mind. He literally shuts the door on learning.

Reading to your child will contribute a great deal to your child's reading ability and success in school. Try to spend at least fifteen minutes a day reading to your child. It is never too soon to begin. An infant will enjoy your voice and looking at the pictures in a book. Observing your enjoyment and pleasure in reading will have a very positive effect on your child's attitude toward reading.

If you have doubts about your child's hearing ability, contact your local board of education and request information on the nearest location for a hearing examination. Once you determine that your child's hearing is normal, his ability to listen can be enhanced by involving him in the listening activities in this section. Many of these activities lend themselves to genuine family fun. Children are fascinated when adults enter enthusiastically into games. This type of activity provides an example to imitate, creates excitement, and helps a child to accept directions.

Learning at home to pay attention, listen, and translate what he hears into action will help your child when he enters an organized play group or starts school.

PASS IT ON

This game improves listening skills and encourages clear speech. As one word passes from person to person, it becomes apparent how important it is to listen, to focus on the spoken word, and to speak clearly.

Materials Needed

None

Activity

All of the members in the family can play. The first person whispers a word to the second, and the second person whispers that same word to the next person, and so on. The last person to hear the word says it aloud—hopefully, it is the same as the original word. Usually, it is different from the original word and the group enjoys noting the difference. Progress to phrases and then to sentences as the players become more proficient.

From *Playing Together, Learning Together*, published by GoodYearBooks.

CHAIN REACTION

This group activity enhances your child's memory and attention span as it develops his ability to concentrate. These thinking skills are essential for everyday school activities and for the rest of life. This family-friendly activity benefits all members, young and old.

 Materials Needed

None

 Activity

The entire family can play this together. One member may snap his fingers, the next person snaps her fingers and claps her hands, the next person snaps his fingers, claps his hands, and taps his feet. Each player must correctly repeat all previous actions in the exact sequence as well as add one at the end. The game can end one of two ways: when one player cannot successfully repeat all the actions, then the other players are all the winners; or if play continues until all but one player is eliminated, he is the winner.

 Variation

Another sequencing game is I Went to the Zoo. The first player would say, "I went to the zoo and saw a lion." The next player might say, "I went to the zoo and saw a lion and a bear." The game continues in the same way as described above. Other sequences could include going to the grocery store, going to the clothing store, or going to a farm.

MUSIC MOODS

Music appreciation should begin at an early age. The different tempos of classical music, for example, inspire certain feelings that your child can express through drawing. This will improve your child's memory and expression. All children respond favorably to music, and the following activity will make music come alive for the child.

Materials Needed

Records, tapes, or CDs of classical music (or any music you prefer); a cassette, record, or CD player; paper and crayons or markers

Activity

Listen with your child to a recording of a classical piece, such as Schubert's Symphony no. 8 in B minor (Unfinished), one of Bach's Brandenburg Concertos, Beethoven's Symphony no. 9, op. 125 (Choral), or Vivaldi's The Four Seasons (four violin concertos). Have your child draw, even scribble, as he listens to the music. Encourage him to make dark lines for loud music and light lines for soft music; to draw rapidly for quick tempos and slowly for slower tempos. Since the emphasis is really on listening and appreciating music, the drawing should be evaluated as an expression of moods and feelings rather than as art.

Talk with your child about what he was feeling while the music played. Have him point out, if he can, features in the drawing that illustrate his moods and feelings. Children love to let themselves "go" completely and respond to the mood of the music. This is a wonderful way to learn to communicate with your child. You will find that your child will readily express his innermost feelings once he understands what you mean by feelings. Talk with him about sad, happy, hurt, lonely, angry, and so on. Before you know it, you will be involved in your child's very own inner thoughts. Always show you care, and take seriously his trust and confidence in talking with you.

Variation

Have your child close his eyes while listening to a particular selection. When the music is over, have him draw a picture of how the music made him feel. An upbeat tempo, for instance, might produce a "happy" drawing.

THE BEAT GOES ON

Moving to the beat helps your child respond to music whether it be classical, popular, jazz, or country.

Materials Needed

Radio or recordings, various household objects

Activity

Five- and six-year-olds enjoy clapping in time to music. This requires concentration. Have an older child bounce a ball to the beat of a song. Create rhythm band instruments using simple items such as a pie tin and spoons (drum), a paper bag partially filled with beans (maracas), pan lids (cymbals), and so on. Many other activities can be done to music: dancing, jumping, and calisthenics like jumping jacks or leg lifts.

MYSTERY INDOOR SOUNDS

A child's environment is filled with many different and wonderful "mystery sounds." Listening to them helps him to distinguish one from another. This early listening trains your child to hear the difference between the sounds of p and t, m and n, d and b, and so on. It is good preparation for learning phonics in school.

Materials Needed

Tape recorder and a tape of household noises and family members' voices

Activity

Record different household sounds (vacuum cleaner, whistling tea kettle, running water, jingling keys, ice cubes being dropped into a glass, brushing teeth, going up and down steps, closing a door, popping popcorn, and so on). Leave a little blank tape between each sound. Play them back one at a time and have your child identify each "mystery sound."

Variation

Record members of the family speaking. Children will enjoy identifying the voices of grandma, grandpa, aunts, and uncles. Have family members try to disguise their voices. Expect more fun and laughter when your child says, "That's Uncle Charlie; I'd know his voice anywhere!" Notice how he has focused his attention on listening intently to the spoken word. Excellent training!

From *Playing Together, Learning Together*, published by GoodYearBooks. Copyright © 1996 Joan Barrett and Linda Thompson.

MYSTERY OUTDOOR SOUNDS

This activity not only helps your child to understand the world around him, it also develops his listening and memory skills. By using a tape recorder your child learns at his own speed. He can play his tape over and over to review what he has learned. He is also learning to appreciate nature and the beauty of the world he is a part of.

Materials Needed

Tape recorder and a tape of collected outdoor sounds

Activity

With a tape recorder, record sounds from various places such as the zoo, airport, shopping center, a parade, or school. In a quiet moment at home when there are no other distractions, listen to the recorded sounds with your child. Encourage him to identify the sounds and where they were recorded. Urge him to express his feelings upon hearing the different sounds. The sound of a marching band may make him happy, while the sound of a lion roaring may be a little frightening. This provides an excellent opportunity for the two of you to communicate.

LISTENING TO RECORDINGS

Listening to recordings of nature and sound effects sensitizes your child to his environment and develops his ability to listen discriminatingly. To distinguish between minor-key selections (usually sad) and major-key selections (usually happy) makes him able to discern differences between sound, music, and just plain noise.

Materials Needed

Record, cassette, or CD player; recordings

Activity

Play seasonal and sound effects recordings such as Environmental Sound Experiences—Solitudes Volume Two, "Ocean Surf in a Hidden Cove" (Dan Gibson Productions Ltd.) and enjoy their truly authentic nature sounds. Sing a Song of Holiday Seasons (Prentice Hall) offers selections from Halloween to Hanukkah. Your child might also enjoy listening to Raffi's upbeat songs in his Everything Grows (A & M Records) album. Tom Chapin's Family Tree offers a wonderful selection of fun songs the whole family can learn and sing together. For a change of pace, try Claude Debussy's La Mer, or The Sea Symphony by Ralph Vaughan Williams. Many of these selections and a variety of others may be found at your local library.

SING-ALONG

This activity will benefit the entire family because a family that sings together, stays together. You can't be angry if you sing together. Encourage singing together anytime, day or night, riding in the car, or picnicking in the park. Just do it, and in no time you'll have a chorus. Singing together develops an appreciation for music and literature. It also contributes to your child's wealth of knowledge and reflects his cultural environment. By singing a nursery rhyme or poem to your child you are broadening his learning capabilities. Singing together enriches his memory, vocabulary, and sense of rhythm. Once the songs become familiar, your child will be able to identify them for the rest of his life. He will be culturally enriched.

Materials Needed

Songs and poems of your choice. Some original songs and music appear on pages 11, 13-14, and 93-94

Activity

Memorize familiar songs and rhymes and sing or recite them together. Choose a short poem and read it often to your child. Have him repeat it to you. Body movements can be coordinated with the words of the songs or rhymes.

Variation

Try singing together the ABCs, days of the week, and months of the year, counting by fives, tens, hundreds, and so on using a familiar tune that you both can follow. Music will hold your child's attention longer than straight memorization. By putting the days of the week, for example, into a song format, your child will not only enjoy the activity, but will also be more likely to remember the information.

"HIGH UP IN THE SKY"

This is a wonderful, sweet, easy-to-sing song with a very important message.

The little girl in the first verse loves watching the diamond-like stars at night. She knows that if she tries very hard at what she wants to do, she can "shine" someday, just like the stars. If you believe in yourself and try very hard you can make anything happen.

The little boy in the second verse loves watching the beautiful butterfly. He realizes there's beauty in the world but also in all of us. All we have to do is reach out and share our smiles and joy with others.

Teach your child this song. Sing it to him often. Soon he will be humming and singing along with you. Talk about the words and ideas in the song to get him thinking about his goals and ambitions.

HIGH UP IN THE SKY
Words and Music By Mary Murphy

1. One day a lit - tle girl watched a
2. One day a lit - tle boy watched a

shim - mer - ing spark - l - ing star so bright
beau - ti - ful col - or - ful but - ter - fly

How she love - d to gaze up at the diamonds in the night
How he love - d to watch the but - ter - fly soar up in the sky

VERSE

High, high, high up in the sky high, high high up in the sky

She sang, I as the star will smile and glow
He sang, I as the butter - fly love to smile

I as the star way up high will know
I as the butter - fly will dance all the while

that if I dream of things I'd like to try I'd
there's so much beau - ty in the world we live, there's

reach for the high - est star in the sky
so much beau - ty in our - selves to give

FINAL ENDING-OPTIONAL

We must al - ways look high up in the sky

and dream of things we'd like to try

"WILLY AND TAFFY"

Sometime between the ages of three and five, children's imaginations go wild. They love to pretend they are firefighters and nurses, moms and dads, dancers and cowpokes. Too often, they are not allowed enough quiet time and the freedom to daydream. Their lives are scheduled, almost programmed. Childhood can and should be a wonderful time in life, without worries, and filled with make believe.

Children often create imaginary friends—as real to them as real people. It's not unusual for a parent or caregiver to set an extra place at a dinner table for a child's play friend. These imaginary friends participate in daily activities and are tucked into bed at night. Along with imaginary friends, children often talk endlessly to their stuffed animals and dolls. Allow them to enjoy this time. All too soon it's over and the real world is upon them.

"Willy and Taffy" is about bears, bunnies, and a very busy family caught up in everyday things.

WILLY AND TAFFY
Words and Music By Patti and Michael Roe

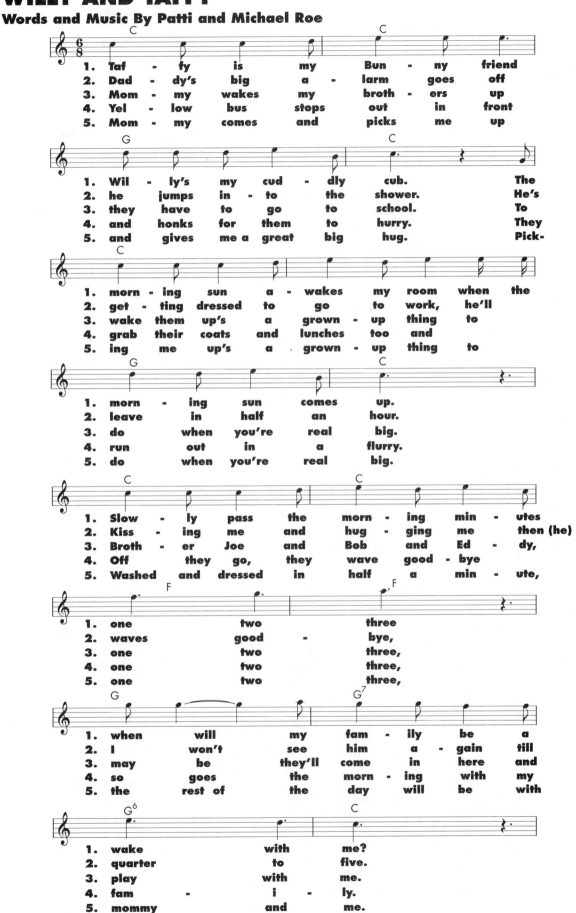

1. Taf - fy is my Bun - ny friend
2. Dad - dy's big a - larm goes off
3. Mom - my wakes my broth - ers up
4. Yel - low bus stops out in front
5. Mom - my comes and picks me up

1. Wil - ly's my cud - dly cub. The
2. he jumps in - to the shower. He's
3. they have to go to school. To
4. and honks for them to hurry. They
5. and gives me a great big hug. Pick-

1. morn - ing sun a - wakes my room when the
2. get - ting dressed to go to work, he'll
3. wake them up's a grown - up thing to
4. grab their coats and lunches too and
5. ing me up's a grown - up thing to

1. morn - ing sun comes up.
2. leave in half an hour.
3. do when you're real big.
4. run out in a flurry.
5. do when you're real big.

1. Slow - ly pass the morn - ing min - utes
2. Kiss - ing me and hug - ging me then (he)
3. Broth - er Joe and Bob and Ed - dy,
4. Off they go, they wave good - bye
5. Washed and dressed in half a min - ute,

1. one two three
2. waves good - bye,
3. one two three,
4. one two three,
5. one two three,

1. when will my fam - ily be a
2. I won't see him a - gain till
3. may be they'll come in here and
4. so goes the morn - ing with my
5. the rest of the day will be with

1. wake with me?
2. quarter to five.
3. play with me.
4. fam - i - ly.
5. mommy and me.

WILLY AND TAFFY

CHORUS:

1. 2. 3. 4. Wil - ly and Taf - fy my
5. Wil - ly and Taf - fy my

bear and my bun - ny
bear and my bun - ny

why must you sit there
thanks for sit - ting there

look - ing so fun - ny?
look - ing so fun - ny.

I'm as a - lone as
I'm just as happy as

lone - ly can be,
hap - py can be,

when will my fam - ily come
here with my Wil - ly, Taffy,

play with me?
mommy and me.

MAKE-BELIEVE

Children learn to speak a language when they associate specific words with identifiable actions. Make-Believe aids your child's recall and retention of the spoken word and develops his imagination and creativity.

Materials Needed

Various nursery rhymes, stories, songs, poems

Activity

While you read a familiar story or poem or sing a favorite song with your child, have him perform the actions it describes. In "Hickory, Dickory, Dock," he could be the mouse climbing up the clock; in "Teddy Bear, Teddy Bear, Turn Around," he could be the teddy bear turning around, touching the ground, and tying his shoe. Children love to pretend to be characters like Peter Pan, Cinderella, Superman, and Little Red Riding Hood. There are endless possibilities with every story or song.

SHAKE 'EM UP

Shake 'Em Up allows children to associate objects and shapes with the unique sounds these shapes make in a container. Sound recognition is an important hallmark of a developed sense of hearing. To recognize objects purely by their sound is the ultimate goal of developing your child's overall auditory system.

Materials Needed

Empty tins or oatmeal boxes, household objects such as marbles, crayons, buttons, coins, rice, popcorn

Activity

Fill two identical tins or boxes with the same objects and a third with a different object. For example, fill two tins with marbles and the third with crayons. Have your child shake all three tins and identify which one makes a different sound. Then, open each one to check which two are filled with the same objects. Change the items in the tins frequently to make it interesting and more fun for your child.

Variation

Have your child identify which tin sounds different and then figure out what objects are in each tin before opening them.

LISTEN TO THE LEADER

This activity allows your child to practice immediate recall of sounds. It develops auditory memory, attention span, and concentration skills as well.

 Materials Needed

Blindfold (optional)

 Activity

This is similar to Following Directions (page 18); however, instead of watching the leader, your child listens to the leader. Have your child close his eyes or wear a blindfold. The leader performs a series of audible actions, such as clapping her hands three times and snapping her fingers twice. For the young child, start with two sounds. An older child could begin with three distinguishing sounds such as clapping hands, stamping feet, and pounding a table. Have your child repeat the exact sequence of sounds in order.

FOLLOWING DIRECTIONS

While strengthening your child's auditory perception, Following Directions challenges him to recall and respond to spoken instructions. This exercise also helps him become more familiar with his body parts and their capabilities.

Materials Needed

None

Activity

When you and your child are alone and there are no other distractions, have him follow a series of directions, such as "Touch your head with your right hand and walk to the door." You should say them only once, and he must not do them until you have finished. When he has completed one sequence, praise him and then give another set of directions: "Touch your left ear with your left hand and skip to the door." Begin with very simple directions. Increase the difficulty after your child has succeeded at the simpler level. Once he understands that he must listen to the entire direction before moving and he becomes really good at the activity he will enjoy playing the game Simon Says. His goal is to be able to remember a complete set of directions. This will train your child to focus on the spoken word, evaluate it, and act upon it. Following directions is so important for your child's academic success.

SEEK AND FIND

This activity improves your child's awareness of detail. His listening and concentration skills, his vocabulary and memory ability are sharpened playing Seek and Find.

 Materials Needed

Any household item

 Activity

Ask your child to bring you a particular object from a large variety of objects such as "my green dress from the closet," "the red-flowered towel in the bathroom," or "the glass with the gold rim from the pantry." Show your pleasure when he follows your instruction. Do not become angry or impatient if he brings the wrong item. Make sure he is not only hearing you, but listening to exactly what you're saying. If he again fails to bring the right object, go with him and find it together. Never discontinue an activity when he feels unsuccessful and unable to please you. It's important that he doesn't perceive himself as a failure. Give older children more than one instruction to follow, but start with simple ones and lead up to the more detailed or difficult.

SHOPPING LISTS

Shopping Lists allows your child to "shop" for items with which he is familiar, using his memory as a list. It also improves your child's vocabulary and encourages him to assume personal responsibility.

Materials Needed

None

Activity

Before you and your child go to the grocery store, tell him the items you need to buy. Initially, give him a short list of three or four items to remember. Have him repeat the list to you. When you arrive at the grocery store, ask your child to recall as many items as possible. If he doesn't remember all of them, give him clues to the ones that he cannot recall. Depending on how well he does, adjust the list for the next shopping trip. If he only remembered three out of six items, give him just three items to recall. Build up from three the next time you venture to the store. It is important to bolster his confidence through his everyday activities!

I SAY HOP

Having to focus on a specific command develops your child's power of concentration and attention. I Say Hop requires an immediate response to the spoken word, enhancing his ability to make correct judgments.

Materials Needed

None

Activity

In this game, the leader gives commands that are to be followed, regardless of what she does. For example, if the leader says, "I say clap your hands" and then she touches her toes, the players must clap their hands. If the leader says, "I say turn around" and then jumps, the players must turn around. Some children will close their eyes so they can listen without the distraction of the leader doing something different than what she says. The child who closes his eyes is focusing completely on the verbal directions. He is training his auditory perception skill, which is exactly the purpose of this activity.

WHAT'S HOT WHAT'S NOT

This activity directs the child to listen and interpret what he hears and to respond to it in a physical way. His attention span, concentration, vocabulary, and expressive language are developed. This also makes an exciting group activity, encouraging children to interact with their playmates in a positive fashion.

Materials Needed

Any object to hide

Activity

Hide an object in a given area. Have the players walk around within the area as you call to them "You're hot" or "You're cold." (Hot means that person is close to the object, cold means he's farther away from the hidden object.) As a player gets very close to the hidden object, use such clues as "You're boiling." Use phrases such as "You're freezing" or "You are getting warmer" depending on a player's closeness to the object.

FRYING VEGETABLES

Playing this game sharpens auditory processing and immediate physical response. A group activity like this helps your child interact in a favorable way with his peers.

Materials Needed

None

Activity

Five or more players sit in a circle with the player designated to be "It" standing in the center. Give each player the name of a vegetable (corn, cabbage, carrots, beans, broccoli, and so on). "It" calls the names of two vegetables. When hearing their names called, those two children try to exchange places while "It" attempts to reach one of their spots before the other can get to it. The player left standing is the new "It" and the game continues. If "It" calls "frying pan turn over," all players must run to a different seat while "It" again tries to reach one of the spots first.

NARÍZ, OJO, OREJA, BOCA

Children learning a foreign language enjoy this game to help with vocabulary development. You can substitute any other language for the Spanish *naríz* (nose), *boca* (mouth), *oreja* (ear), and *ojo* (eye). This is a delightful, quick, and easy way to familiarize children with some basic words used in other languages.

Materials Needed

None

Activity

Players sit in a straight line in front of the leader who faces the group. The leader taps her nose and says, "naríz, naríz, naríz" while all the others imitate her. On the next word, boca, the leader taps her ear or some feature other than her mouth, to confuse the group. The players must touch their mouths when the word boca is spoken. If a player makes a mistake, he then becomes the leader. With young children, begin by using just two new words. Add other body part words to the game as they are learned. Play the game rapidly.

Pronunciation Guide

Naríz = nah RÉES

Boca = BÓH ka

Ojo = ÓHO

Oreja = or ÉH ha

  From *Playing Together, Learning Together*, published by GoodYearBooks. Copyright © 1996 Joan Barrett and Linda Thompson.

LEARNING TO SEE

A child's eyes need special practice to learn to move in preparation for reading. Practice in eye movement is absolutely essential for any degree of success in the classroom. If you doubt your child's ability to see well, take her to a qualified ophthalmologist. Your local board of health, Lion's Club, or Easter Seals organization can direct you to a doctor or clinic that will provide qualified service free or at a minimal cost. Once it is determined that your child's sight is adequate, you can help develop her visual skills by engaging her in the activities in this section.

The ultimate learning skill is that of visual memory. Like listening, it is a learned ability and not inherent. The recall and visualization of previous experiences furnish a background against which every new experience can be evaluated by the child. If these reference points are not available to a child for visualized comparisons, she will fail to understand relationships, associations, sequencing, order, and many of the other factors that must be weighed and judged in every learning activity.

Start with the very simple activities and proceed to the more difficult ones. Be careful not to burden your child with too difficult an activity as it will only frustrate her and create a sense of defeat. She must *feel* she can do a task before she can do it. Confidence is one of the most important traits that you can help develop in your child. Limit yourself to short periods of time so that your child's attention and interest remain high. When you see her tiring, either change the activity or resume it another day. It is better to work for short periods of time more often than to work for long periods of time less often.

STORY REWRITE

This activity enables your child to use her imagination and develop her logical thought process. Being able to think and talk is the essence of life. If you live in a nonverbal world, you limit yourself to a very small circle of people. Story Rewrite also helps your child to visualize outcomes.

Materials Needed

Children's books, correction fluid, masking tape

Activity

Locate an old Mother Goose book or Little Golden Book that your child has enjoyed but may be ready to trade in. Give the book a new life and create hours of enjoyment. With typewriter correction fluid or masking tape, cover a variety of key words in the story—characters' names, places, and so on. Now you and your child can develop a new story. Write the words in as your child relates them to you. ("Mary had a little lamb" could become "Jimmy had a little dog." The "Wizard of Oz" could be "The Dragon of Op.") Encourage her to use her imagination vigorously. After you have finished filling in the new information, you or your child can read the "new story." Not only does this give life to an old book, but it helps your child realize that reading and writing can be so much fun! Begin with short stories or poems. An older child may wish to tackle longer ones.

REMEMBER THE PICTURE

The ability to look at something and remember its details is important in everyday life. Becoming aware and being alert are good characteristics to develop. Remember the Picture also helps improve your child's memory.

 Materials Needed

Magazines

 Activity

Look through magazines for a fun picture. Briefly show your child the picture. After removing it from his sight, ask her to name three items in the picture. The number of items you request and the kind of information you ask for depend on your child's ability. Always begin at a level that she can handle and then progress to the more difficult. If necessary, show her the picture one more time. Make sure you praise her for her efforts! Be sure to finish the game when she has had success in naming the items in the picture. If she cannot remember four, go back to three or two items and then call an end to the game.

PICTURE ADS

"Reading" pictures is an essential step in learning to read words. Observing detail and discerning similarities and differences in pictures help to develop the skill of visual discrimination, or being able to distinguish differences between printed letters (such as p and q, n and m, and d and b).

Materials Needed

Newspapers or magazines

Activity

With your child, peruse the illustrated ads in newspapers and magazines. Compare different types of shoes (high-heeled or low, dressy or sandals), clothing (dress clothes or sport clothes), toys, and so on. In the real estate section, compare the different types of homes pictured. By making these observations, the child becomes aware of differences in her everyday environment.

From *Playing Together, Learning Together,* published by GoodYearBooks. Copyright © 1996 Joan Barrett and Linda Thompson.

DISAPPEARING ACT

This activity strengthens your child's memory and her ability to note detail, which are fundamental in learning to read and write.

Materials Needed

Several household objects

Activity

While doing dishes and enjoying each other's company, put an arrangement of objects on the table such as a cup, fork, spoon, napkins, and plate. Have your child look at the collection for a short period of time. With a younger child, start with just two items and ask the child to name them. Ask your child to look away while you remove one item. When she turns back, have her recall which item is missing. Increase the number of objects when your child has succeeded at the previous level. Let your child have a turn at removing an item for you to recall!

WHAT'S MISSING?

Helping your child to understanding the relationship of a part to its whole and enhancing her visual memory are the goals of this activity. Playing this game also increases your child's awareness of her immediate environment.

Materials Needed

Toys with removable pieces: dolls and doll clothes, model cars or trucks

Activity

When your child plays with dolls, make a game of removing one article of clothing when she is not looking and then having your child determine what was removed. Remove more than one article at a time if your child can easily identify one missing piece. This activity can also be played with other toys that have removable pieces.

COMIC STRIPS

This activity provides a wonderful opportunity to develop your child's thinking abilities. It also helps her see cause and effect in relationships, to sequence, and to note significant detail.

Materials Needed

Newspapers, scissors

Activity

Help your child select a comic strip from the newspaper. Read it together, discussing the pictures and the characters—what they are doing, why they're doing it. Challenge her imagination by asking questions such as "What do you think happened after the last frame in the comic strip?" Good thinking habits can be best learned from you with plenty of give and take. Even the youngest child has ideas to bring out and listen to. Then cut apart each frame of the cartoon and ask your child to arrange them in their original order.

Variation

Make the activity more difficult for an older child by cutting up a comic strip before discussing it and having her sequence it properly.

FIND THE HIDDEN OBJECTS

Eye pursuit activities of this kind help your child learn to focus on specifics. To be able to sort out meaningful from nonessential information is necessary to accomplish everyday tasks. Being involved with other players in this game helps your child develop social skills.

Materials Needed

Bottle tops, buttons, pencils, crayons, coins, or other easily manipulated items

Activity

Vary the Easter egg hunt idea by scattering bottle caps on the grass and asking your children and friends to find them. The winner gathers the most in a given time. You could also scatter buttons or candies in a room in your house, making sure you know how many you started with!

Variation

If you really want to generate high interest in a group of children, try this variation of the game. Scatter wood chips in a blocked-off area. Plant a variety of coins (pennies, nickels, dimes, quarters) and give the signal to hunt. Stand back and watch them scramble!

PUZZLE TIME

Manipulating puzzle pieces reinforces your child's ability to visualize a completed picture and exercises her coordination.

Materials Needed

Magazines, scissors, paste, cardboard

Activity

Look through a magazine with your child and find a picture that interests her. Carefully remove it from the magazine and paste it on a heavy piece of cardboard. Then cut it into as many pieces as your child can easily manipulate and reassemble. Increase or decrease the number of pieces in the puzzle depending on your child's success. Start with the picture puzzle on page 34 of this book if you wish.

Finished Picture

MATCH GAME

Match Game encourages attention to detail and helps improve your child's ability to focus on a given task. Awareness of similarities and differences begins with this simple activity.

Materials Needed

Paper or activity sheets (pages 36-38), pencil

Activity

Draw a symbol or geometric figure on the left side of a piece of paper. Then draw a series of different symbols in a horizontal row next to the original, including one exactly the same as the original. Ask your child to find the one that matches the original. Be sure to draw objects that are familiar to your child to help capture her attention. When first doing this activity, make the drawings simple, so that the similar figures stand out. Once your child has mastered the simple drawings, gradually proceed to more complicated ones. For examples, see activity sheets on pages 36-38.

MATCH GAME

3 to 5 Year Olds

MATCH GAME

5 to 7 Year Olds

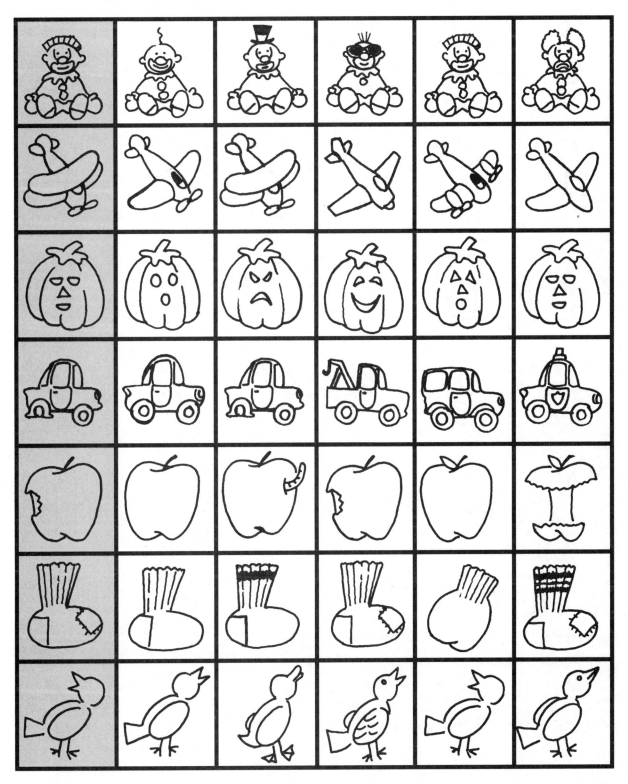

MATCH GAME

7 to 9 Year Olds

STICKER FUN

This activity focuses on attention to detail and helps improve your child's listening skills and concentration level.

Materials Needed

Paper or activity sheet (page 40), package of stickers

Activity

Purchase a package of stickers from your local card store or supermarket, making sure your package has four or five sheets. Each page of stickers should be exactly the same, so you'll have four or five of each design. Select stickers that will have the most appeal for your child. Begin by using the activity sheet on page 40 or make one of your own. You may want to start with only two or three stickers in each row, depending on your child's ability level. Choose a specific sticker and ask your child to peel it off and place it in the first box. Then ask her to place five more stickers in the next five boxes. Of those five, ask for four different stickers and one that is exactly the same as the first sticker in that row. After you have filled up three or four rows (or the entire page), have your child find the stickers that match exactly in each row. Now let her do the same with you.

STICKER FUN

PAIRING UP

You can use a deck of cards to help your child develop in many areas. Number concepts, similarities and differences, greater than and less than, sequencing, and awareness of colors and shapes (diamonds, hearts, clubs, spades) can all be practiced and strengthened.

Materials Needed

Deck of cards

Activity

This quick little game should be fun for the two of you. It is a start in teaching your child to concentrate and keep her mind on a task. From a deck of cards, select several pairs. Mix them up and lay them face down on a table. The first player turns over two cards. If they are alike, she keeps the pair and continues her turn until turning over two different cards. If they are not alike, she puts the cards back in their original place face down and the next player tries to make a match. The player with the most pairs wins the game. Be sensitive to your child's capabilities. For a younger child, begin with just two pairs of cards. Add more pairs and more players as your child becomes more proficient. This can be a fun group or family activity.

Variation

See Coupon Craze, page 42.

COUPON CRAZE

Today's children are exposed to so much visual stimuli in the form of advertising that it needs to be put to their advantage. It is not unusual, for example, to hear a two- or three-year-old looking out the car window say, "There's McDonald's," or "There's Dairy Queen." She is developing her own sight vocabulary. Using familiar advertising, Coupon Craze helps promote your child's awareness of detail, expands her vocabulary, and improves her memory. It also makes her feel part of the adult world.

Materials Needed

Newspaper or magazine coupon ads, index cards, glue

Activity

One fun way to do this is with the coupons that are available in newspapers, grocery stores, and on your doorstep. Go through newspapers or magazines together looking for brightly colored coupons with words your child recognizes. The whole family can become coupon collectors! To play this game, you will need to locate twelve pairs of identical coupons. After you have found them, paste them individually onto index cards so that they will be easier to handle. The game requires four players. Show the coupons to all the players. Talk about the coupons. Have your child become familiar with the names of the twelve pairs. Shuffle the cards and deal six coupon cards to each of the four players. The first player (the dealer) lays down all matching pairs of cards from his hand, reading the names (if possible). The next three players in turn do the same. The first player (dealer) then takes any two cards from his hand and passes them to the player on his left. That second player then matches up like coupons (if any) and puts them on the table. She then passes two of her cards to the player on her left. Continue around the table passing two cards to the left and matching paired coupons. Play continues until someone runs out of cards. The player with the most matches wins.

Variation

These coupon cards could be used to play the game Pairing Up on page 41. The number of cards you use depends, of course, on the age of your child.

YELLOW BRICK ROAD

Staying within two parallel lines involves visual perception and visual motor coordination. Developing and strengthening the small muscles in the hands are essential in learning how to write.

Materials Needed

Sample activity sheets on pages 44 and 45, paper, pencil

Activity

For a young child, draw two parallel lines about two inches apart across a page and draw or paste a figure on the left-hand side between the parallel lines and a related figure on the right (for example, a mouse and a piece of cheese). Repeat for the length of the page. Have your child draw a line from the figure on the left-hand side to the related figure on the right-hand side, trying not to touch either parallel line. For the five- to six-year-old child, place a picture in the upper left-hand corner and related picture at the bottom right. Draw the two parallel lines from one to the other in a winding fashion. The child should begin at the top left and draw a line to the bottom right, keeping her pencil between the parallel lines. This helps train the eyes to "read" from left to right. Use the same activity for an older child, but narrow the path of the parallel lines. Although this seems like a simple activity, it can be very tiring for the child as it requires constant concentration. Discontinue when she shows signs of tiring and praise her for her good work. Let your child think of pairs of pictures to include in this activity (cow-barn, car-garage, dog-bone, ice cream-cone, and so on). Refer to the sample activity sheets on pages 44 and 45 for more ideas.

YELLOW BRICK ROAD

3 to 4 Year Olds

Bird

Tree

Mouse

Cheese

Fish

Lake

Horse

Barn

YELLOW BRICK ROAD

5 to 6 Year Olds

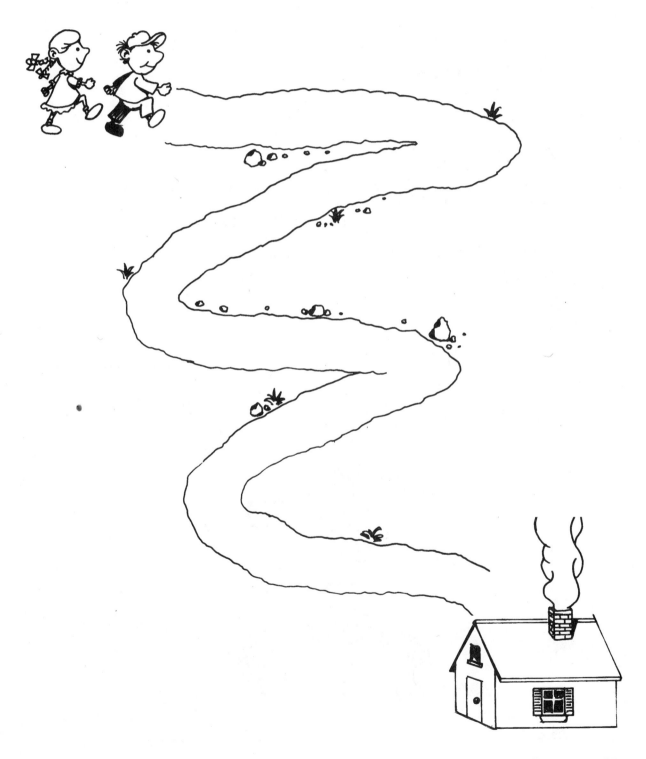

IN-LINE SKATING
RACE FOR TWO

This activity allows your child to improve her coordination, to anticipate a goal, and to enjoy a challenging race with you. This enhances your communication in a most enjoyable way.

Materials Needed

Activity sheets (pages 47 and 48), pencils

Activity

Your older child will enjoy racing with you. On the following pages are two identical mazes, one for each of you. Each contestant starts with twenty points. Work your way down the roller path to the finish line without bumping into any walls, stumbling over stones, or falling in any holes. Each mishap costs you a point. Keep going over the path, up to three times, until one of you is out of points. The one finishing with the most points—even one—is the winner. Have fun! Keep practicing—practice makes perfect.

 Holes

 Stones

IN-LINE SKATING
RACE FOR TWO

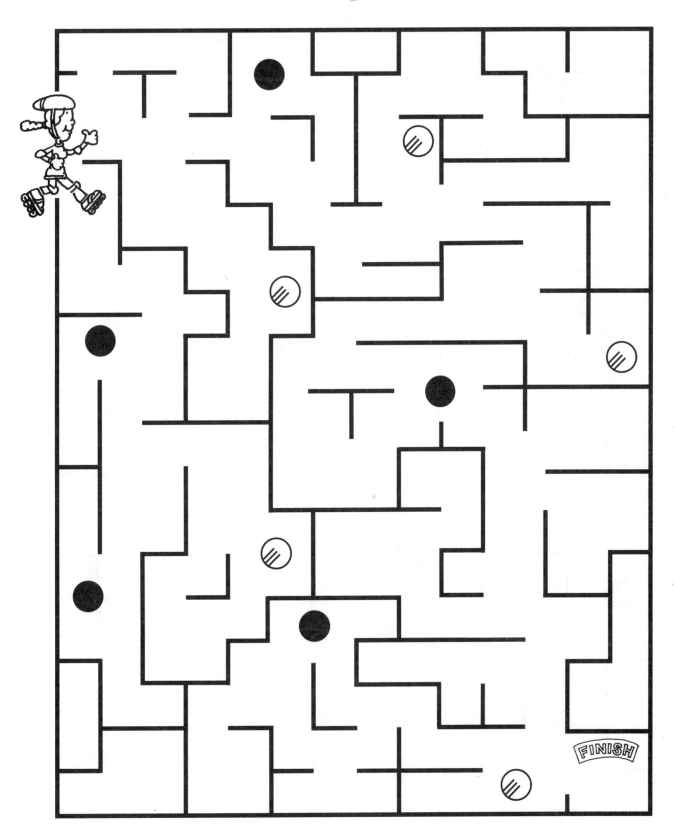

FINISH

IN-LINE SKATING
RACE FOR TWO

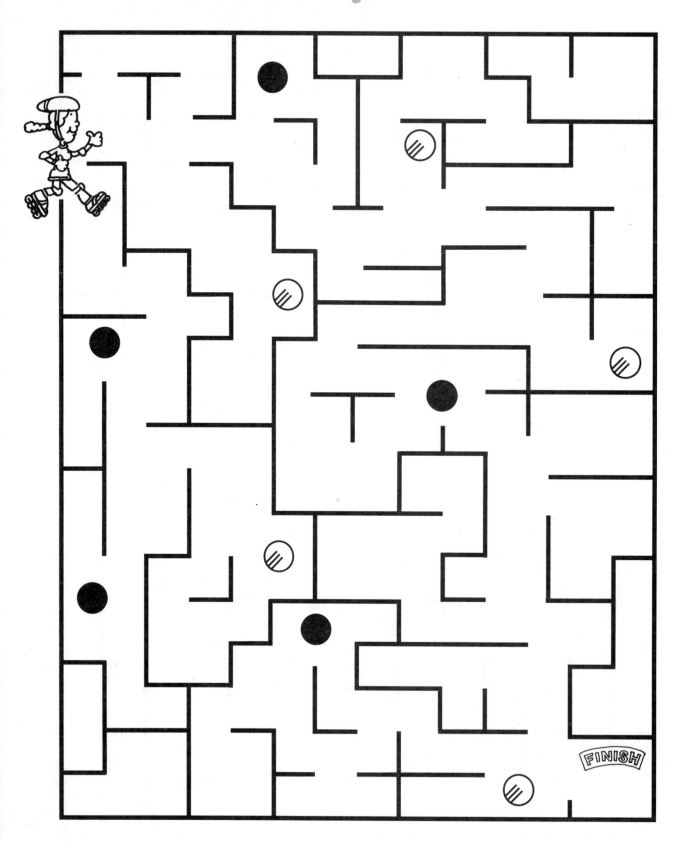

From *Playing Together, Learning Together*, published by GoodYearBooks. Copyright © 1996 Joan Barrett and Linda Thompson.

DOT-TO-DOT

Your child's eye-hand coordination and ability to predict will benefit from Dot-to-Dot. Connecting the dots also develops skills required for learning to write.

Materials Needed

Paper, pencil or crayon, marker, activity sheets (pages 50-52)

Activity

For the younger child, use a large felt-tipped marker and place a number of "dots" randomly on a plain sheet of paper. Have your child practice connecting the dots making sure her pencil or crayon touches each dot before proceeding to the next one. You could also place the dots to form a shape such as a square, triangle, or diamond. Have your child identify the shape once she has connected the dots. Depending on the age of your child, you could then progress to numbering or lettering the dots, encouraging her to connect them in the proper order. The younger to middle child may be able to connect a simple drawing alphabetically while the middle to older child could connect dots that follow a mathematical sequence (counting by fives, tens, and so on). See sample activity sheets on pages 50-52.

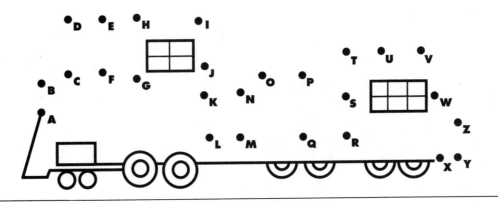

DOT-TO-DOT

3 to 5 Year Olds

•₆

•₅   •₄   •₈
            •₁

•₇

•₃   •₂

Tree

DOT-TO-DOT

5 to 7 Year Olds

•₂

•₃ •₄ ━━━━━━━━━━━━ •₁₁ •₁

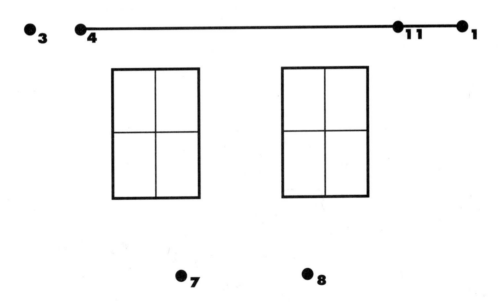

•₇   •₈

•₅   •₆ ━━━━ •₉   •₁₀

House

DOT-TO-DOT

7 to 9 Year Olds

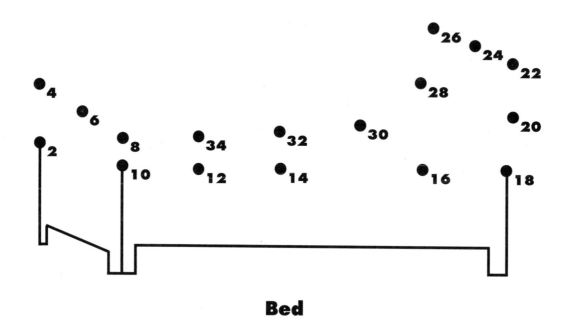

Bed

Alphabet Train

FILL THE GAP

This activity develops left-to-right progression. It also reinforces your child's letter and number concepts and sequencing.

Materials Needed

Paper, pencil

Activity

This particular activity is designed for the middle to older child (depending on her capabilities) who knows the alphabet and understands the ideas of *before* and *after* in a sequence. Begin by writing a segment of the alphabet on a paper, omitting a letter in the series (a, b, c, __), (n, o, p, __), (j, k, __, m). Have your child fill in the missing letter. If your child is familiar with numbers and counting, have her "fill the gap" of a number pattern (3, 4, 5, __), (17, 18, 19, __), (38, __, 40, 41). Challenge older children with more difficult patterns (20, 22, __, 26, 28), (30, 60, 65, 70), (80, 79, 78, __). As always, begin at a level you feel your child can easily handle. If she is too frustrated or does not understand, either explain again carefully or wait until later when she is more ready.

SORTING FUN

People learn by comparing, grouping, and classifying in categories by similarities and differences. Giving your child every opportunity to perform these types of activities establishes her basis for learning.

Materials Needed

Toys, silverware, linens, clothes closet, books, cassette tapes, jewelry

Activity

Your child can help you perform many sorting tasks throughout the day by putting away the dinnerware with the knives, forks and spoons in the appropriate sections; arranging the linen closet by towel size or color; organizing the clothes closet by keeping the skirts, blouses, pants, and so on together; and even picking up toys by type or color. If this activity is presented in a playful manner with you joining in, it can be exciting rather than a chore. You can put the dishes away while he sorts the silverware. See who finishes first. Express your pleasure in having things orderly. External order will facilitate the child's development of an internal sense of order. This purposeful activity and obvious accomplishment gives him a feeling of a "job well done." An older child can rearrange the books by book type (mystery, historical, science-fiction, and so on). or classify the cassette tapes or compact discs (classical, country, and so on).

GRAB BAG

This activity improves small-muscle development in your child's hands. Grab Bag also helps to improve her memory and develop her vocabulary and expressive language.

Materials Needed

Various household objects and a paper or plastic bag

Activity

Gather together several household objects (crayon, pencil, apple, orange, quarter, bottle cap, and so on). Show your child each item and discuss it (size, texture, shape) as you place it in the bag. After all of the objects are in the bag, have your child reach in and identify one without looking. Ask her to describe the object to you. If necessary, ask questions to encourage her. Then she should remove the item to make sure her guess is correct.

Variation

For an older child, place objects in the bag while she is not looking. Have her reach into the bag, feel the objects, and describe and identify each one at a time.

SCRAMBLE

The importance of left-to-right progression, which this game develops, cannot be understated. Your child's eyes must move smoothly from left to right in order to read and write. Scramble also strengthens your child's memory and spelling skills.

Materials Needed

Magazines, newspapers, scissors, paper, pencil

Activity

This activity is for the child who already recognizes and is familiar with the letters of the alphabet. Cut out headline letters from a magazine or newspaper. Form a word with these letters, pointing to each letter and saying each one aloud. For later reference, write that word on a separate piece of paper or card. Then scramble the letters and have her arrange them in the correct order. She should then check to see if she is correct. Begin with two- or three-letter words depending upon your child's capabilities. This is a fun way to test the spelling skills of an older child. Let your child have a turn letting you unscramble a word.

Variation

For a somewhat more challenging memory game, form nonsense words to have your child remember, making sure you write the original "word" down on the separate piece of paper or card.

LET'S GET PHYSICAL

Physical skills are the first kind of skills that children demonstrate. Playing ball does not contribute in a direct way to knowledge; however, it does develop the large-muscle system and contributes to overall fitness. In addition, participating in gross motor activities and interacting with playmates are wonderful ways to learn social skills and secure peer relationships. Encourage your child to do as many physical activities as possible: ice skating, roller skating, tennis, bowling, football, badminton, walking, skipping, running, and soccer. These activities not only develop muscles and eye-hand coordination, they also encourage self-discipline and self-respect.

Evidence has proved that participating in games will motivate children to learn concepts related to reading and to language. In several studies, James H. Humphrey (1974) demonstrated that children taught various languages with an "active game method" learned significantly more than the control group taught using the traditional medium of a language workbook. Moderate exercise reduces excess tensions and stress, thereby contributing to efficient mental work. Building and strengthening body muscles, and improving eye-hand coordination and overall physical fitness helps to develop the "whole" child, physically, emotionally, and mentally.

Hands, especially, need practice in learning to move in preparation for penmanship. Fine motor activities develop small muscles in the hands. The "feel" of size and shape must match the "look" of size and shape. Texture, temperature, weight, hardness, and softness must be appraised and appreciated by both the hands and the visual systems, or eye-hand coordination will not develop as it must for skill in learning.

MINI-TASKS

Mini-tasks develop fine-motor skills and build your child's self-confidence. Be patient with his early attempts at these simple, daily tasks and always remember your child learns by doing.

Materials Needed

Shoes and laces, buttons, zippers, light switches, needle and thread, hammer and nail, and other similar household "mini-task" items

Activity

Since children learn by doing, encourage your young child to button his own buttons, lace his own shoes, and zip his zippers, as well as turn the lights, radio, and TV on and off. Of course, this may require considerable patience on your part. An older child can lock and unlock doors, thread a needle, hammer a nail, or seal and stamp envelopes. Mastering simple tasks can aid in mastering slightly more complicated tasks such as cross stitch, woodworking, and other crafts and hobbies. Remember to keep the projects simple at first and praise your child's every attempt. What seems simple to you may be monumental to him.

LACE IT

Along with eye-hand coordination, a strong sense of accomplishment is a benefit of this activity. Display the finished product on the refrigerator or door for everyone to admire.

Materials Needed

Cardboard, hole punch, yarn or shoe laces, coloring book or paper, pencil

Activity

Glue the bus on the activity sheet (page 60) to cardboard. Punch holes around the perimeter of the bus. Tie a knot in one end of yarn, or tape the end to the back of the bus. Put tape around the other end of the yarn to simulate a needle. Have your child pull the loose end through from the back to the front and lace around the design until he's completed it. Make sure it is finished on the back so you can tie, knot, or tape the yarn. Ask your child to draw people in the bus. Are some people waving? Do they have hats or caps on? Can your child make one person a driver? How might he decorate the bus? Is there advertising on the bus? Make it an enjoyable activity for both of you. Sing "The people on the bus" together. A simple activity such as this can be a really enjoyable experience.

60

SHOE IN

Shoe In develops muscles, eye-hand coordination, and self-reliance.

Materials Needed

A shoe, two different colored laces, and one pair of regular shoelaces

Activity

Lacing a shoe requires the ability to put a lace in a hole and pull it out. It means working with two laces from side to side. To simplify the process, tie together two laces of different colors (white and black) and of equal length at the bottom two holes of a shoe. Tie them so they cannot slip through the first holes. As you work with your child say, "first the white one, then the black one, over and under and through" and so on. When he can do this well with the two laces of different colors, have him work with a same-colored pair of shoelaces. This activity takes time and patience for both of you. It won't be accomplished in one day. Tell him you know it is a difficult task and praise him for each little effort. He might forget how to do it by tomorrow. Show him how to get started and guide him.

SURPRISE BUTTON BOARD

This activity helps to strengthen the small muscles in the hand which are necessary for learning how to write. Surprise Button Board also develops your child's ability to take care of himself. Buttoning and unbuttoning his clothes is a big step in his independence. The exercise also reinforces concentration, patience, eye-hand coordination, and fine-motor skills.

 ## Materials Needed

Piece of board or sturdy cardboard, cardigan sweater or vest, interesting pictures from magazines, paste

 ## Activity

Paste an interesting picture on a smooth piece of board or very sturdy cardboard. (The size depends on the size of clothing you use in the next step.) Fit an old button-down vest or sweater around the board, centering the buttons down the middle. The child should then try to unbutton the sweater to see the picture inside. Have him try to button the sweater as well. Change the pictures often to stimulate his desire to practice. This will take patience for both of you, but he will get better with practice.

CREATIVE ART

In addition to developing the muscles in the hands, this activity provides your child with an opportunity for self-expression. Art helps to improve eye-hand coordination, essential to pre-writing skills.

Materials Needed

Crayons, markers, pens, non-toxic paints, paper, glue, empty medicine bottle with dropper, scissors, yarn, buttons, lace, ribbon, pasta, bottle tops, construction paper or posterboard

Activity

Coloring, painting, drawing, tracing, cutting, and pasting are fun and can provide hours of fine-motor practice. Take the time to do artwork with your child. Use a variety of media such as chalk, markers, crayons, finger paints, and so on. (See Homemade Finger Paint recipe on page 66.) Instead of using paint brushes, try toothbrushes, cotton swabs, sponges, or block printing (page 68). Fill a medicine bottle with paint and use an eye dropper to create a design on paper. Even an empty roll-on deodorant bottle can be used to create art. Pry off the ball and collar on the bottle with a dull knife. Wash out the inside and fill it with liquid tempera paint to make easel painting much neater. Encourage the child to tell you about his work. Remember to respect whatever he draws, giving him support and encouragement. Displaying your child's work will encourage him as well as give him additional self-confidence.

RAINBOW BRIGHT

This activity develops your child's creativity and instills an appreciation for color and blending of colors.

Materials Needed

Coffee filters, paper towels, food coloring or old medicine bottles (with droppers) filled with non-toxic paint

Activity

Moisten a coffee filter or paper towel. Drop various food colors on the damp paper and observe how the colors combine to make new colors. A brilliant, colorful montage emerges. You may also wish to fill old medicine bottles (with droppers) with paint to use for this activity. (See Creative Art, page 63.)

WHAT IS IT?

It is important for your child to listen and to follow directions. This activity develops his imagination and attention to detail, as well as his memory and fine-motor coordination.

Materials Needed

Paper, pencil, crayons or markers

Activity

Describe a person familiar to your child for him to draw: "Draw a picture of a person who wears a blue uniform and hat and carries a mailbag." After your child has finished drawing his picture, check to see if he has drawn a letter carrier. The emphasis is not on how well he draws the picture, but on his ability to follow the directions and to recall details. Did he color the uniform blue? Is the mailbag in the picture? Another example might be, "Draw a picture of a large animal that has four legs, a long trunk, and big ears." After listening to your description, your child should draw an elephant. Begin with simple descriptions of objects or people that are familiar to your child. Allow him the opportunity to describe an object for you to draw.

HOMEMADE FINGER PAINT

Here's an inexpensive way to make your own finger paint.

Materials Needed

1/2 cup powdered laundry starch
1/2 cup cold water
1 cup boiling water
1 tablespoon vinegar
Package of food coloring containing 4 small bottles
4 empty jars
Enamel or formica surface covered with plastic, wet shelf, or butcher paper

Activity

Mix powdered laundry starch and cold water until well blended. Add boiling water and vinegar and mix well. Heat, stirring constantly to boiling point. Cool and add food coloring. (This recipe can be doubled for additional finger paint.) Put a few drops of food coloring into each container and let your child stir with his finger and decide when the desired shade is reached. (He'll love doing this!) Start with the primary colors: red, blue, yellow. The food coloring box that you purchase may also contain green. Let your child discover that red and yellow make orange; blue and yellow make green; red and blue make purple; and red, blue, and yellow make brown. He'll be surprised to discover that mixing green with any of the other colors doesn't make a new color. He's learned that mixing primary colors with others creates entirely new colors. What a discovery for him to enjoy and share with you! Now by moving his hands around on the painted surface, he can create swirls or lines or whatever pattern he desires. Let his imagination go wild to create animals, birds rainbows, and people. Formica surfaces are safe for finger painting, as they wipe clean with a wet rag. The finger paint spreads more easily if the surface is wet, and if he paints on wet shelf or butcher paper, he can hang it up for display when it dries.

STRING SQUIGGLES

Using various materials your child experiences the many possibilities of creativity.

Materials Needed

Lengths of string, yarn, twine, shoelaces, ribbons, gauze

Activity

Give your child two- to three-inch lengths of string, yarn, twine, shoelaces, ribbons, and so on to dip in paint. Finger paint or any available paint will do. Let the excess paint drip off and have him drop the painted string onto a piece of wet paper. Do the same with the rest of the string or yarn. Very young children enjoy doing this, as they are sometimes hesitant about putting their hands directly into finger paint. Once they've become accustomed to this activity, they are more willing to move on into finger painting. When he has dropped all the materials onto the paper and it dries, an interesting work of art emerges. Hang it up and praise your child for a job well done.

BLOCK PRINTING

This activity enhances your child's creative expression and imagination. Block Printing also helps develop the small muscles in your child's hands.

Materials Needed

Potato, pencil, knife, newspapers, dish, berry ink

Activity

Cut a potato in half horizontally. Have your child draw a design on each half of the potato with a pencil. The actual pencil marks will be difficult to see, but encourage him to press hard so that the indentations will be visible. Please do this next part of the activity for your child: Using the point of a sharp knife, "trace around" the design. Then cut away the potato around the design to a depth of one-quarter to one-half inch. The design will be higher than the background. Spread newspaper on a table. Pour into a dish about a half-inch of berry ink. (See Berry Ink recipe, page 69.) The ink should be quite thick. Press the potato "block" into the ink and dab it once or twice on the newspaper. Then press it onto the paper to make an interesting design. These prints can be made on tissue paper to use later for wrapping gifts, on construction paper or posterboard, or to make greeting cards. (See page 70.)

BERRY INK RECIPE

Use this natural ink to make block prints.

Materials Needed

1 cup berries (blueberries, blackberries, strawberries, or raspberries)
Strainer
Small bowl
Spoon
1 teaspoon vinegar
1 teaspoon salt
Small jar with lid

Activity

Place the berries a few at a time in a strainer. Holding the strainer over a small bowl, crush the berries with the back of a spoon so that the juice drips into a bowl. The skin, seeds, and pulp of the berries will remain in the strainer. Discard them and crush a few more berries, repeating the process until all of the berries have been juiced. Next, add vinegar and salt to the berry juice and stir until the salt dissolves. If the color is too pale, add a drop of red or blue food coloring. Pour "ink" into a small jar. When not in use, be sure to keep the lid on the jar. Unfortunately, berry ink won't last long, so make it a little at a time. When it starts to harden, throw it away.

GREETING CARDS

Making greeting cards to send to friends or relatives is a wonderful way for your child to do something thoughtful for others while developing an ability to express himself. This activity also will help improve your child's fine-motor skills through cutting, pasting, coloring, and other manual activities.

 ## Materials Needed

Paper, chalk, paint, crayons, scissors, ribbon, paper doilies, block printing supplies (see page 68)

 ## Activity

Using any kind of paper, allow your child to create an appropriate greeting card for a friend or family member. Whether it be a holiday, birthday, or a get-well wish, your child can design and perhaps even write the verse on his original card. If your child is too young to write, have him tell you what to write. He can decorate his original greeting card with a block printing design. (See Block Printing, page 68.) Don't forget to mail the card!

STEP-BY-STEP

Reading and following directions for various projects reinforces your child's memory, sequencing ability, and coordination.

Materials Needed

Directions and materials for baking cookies, building a model or other craft project, making puppets and dough creations. (For dough activities, see pages 73-75)

Activity

Give your child every opportunity to follow directions for completing projects like baking cookies (and other recipes), cutting out and assembling patterns for clothes, or building birdhouses or model planes and cars. Have him attempt to carry out the directions with your supervision. Make these activities fun so he doesn't feel that it is drudgery or work. If he tires, allow him to continue it later or abandon it and go to a less complicated project.

DOUGH ART

Squeezing and manipulating dough provides finger exercise and sensory pleasure, and helps to develop the smaller muscles in the hands. Dough activities will also strengthen your child's eye-hand coordination, which is essential for learning to write. Your child will enjoy making the dough respond to his touch. As he becomes more familiar with clay or dough the more creative he will become, and pride in his own creative work will enhance his self-esteem. The next few pages suggest a variety of activities with dough.

PLAY DOUGH

Materials Needed

1 cup flour
1/2 cup salt
2 teaspoons cream of tartar
1 cup water
2 tablespoons oil

Activity

Heat oil in saucepan. Mix other ingredients and then add to heated oil and cook for three minutes, stirring constantly. Drop the ball of dough on waxed paper or foil and let it cool enough to handle. Have your child knead the dough until it is smooth and pliable. Separate the ball into smaller portions. Add food coloring to each portion as desired. Enjoy kneading and shaping the dough with your child. Between uses, store the dough in a covered plastic container in the refrigerator. It will keep for two to three weeks.

ORNAMENT DOUGH

Materials Needed

1 cup flour
1/3 cup salt
6 - 8 tablespoons water

Activity

Mix ingredients together, adding water a tablespoon at a time and using only enough to work the flour and salt into a pliable mass. With your child roll out or pat out the dough to a quarter- or half-inch thickness. Let him cut it with cookie cutters or mold designs with his hands. Pierce each ornament at the top with a toothpick to make a hole that can be threaded for hanging after baking. Put the cut-out pieces on a cookie sheet and bake in the oven at 300° until hard. Your child will enjoy painting the ornaments with watercolors or acrylics after they have cooled. Finally, cover the items with several coats of clear spray or liquid varnish.

From *Playing Together, Learning Together*, published by GoodYearBooks. Copyright © 1996 Joan Barrett and Linda Thompson.

BREADSTICK DOUGH

Materials Needed

Tube of breadstick dough

Activity

Purchase a tube of breadsticks found in the refrigerator section of your supermarket containing six or ten strips. (This activity can be used in conjunction with the Big Helper Dinner on page 100.) Have children use the strips of dough to make symbols that relate to their ethnic backgrounds. A Star of David or Saint Lucia wreath can easily be made with the strips. A simple five-pointed star familiar to many ethnic groups can be formed. You'll find children happy to talk about their individual creations, and it is amazing how aware small children are of the origins and significance of their symbols.

Following the directions on the tube, pop the breadstick creations in the oven at 400°, and in eight to ten minutes, you'll have a nutritious snack or accompaniment to a salad for all to enjoy. This learning experience helps children to understand and appreciate the people with whom they share the world.

ORIGAMI

An excellent fine-motor activity, making origami gives your child practice in keeping his mind on a task and following directions.

Materials Needed

Paper, scissors

Activity

Origami is the art of folding and cutting paper into various shapes. It can range from very simple to very complex. You will want to begin this activity with your child very simply. Allow the young child who may not be able to cut successfully to tear or fringe the paper. After practice with this, have him try cutting across a thick line before trying to cut actual shapes. Even if he doesn't "master" cutting, he can still tear a shape or design upon your instruction. For the middle or older child, try giving a simple direction to folding the paper In half to make a heart, for example, or a circle. You may want to use different types of paper, including typing or construction paper, gift wrap, or even aluminum foil. If your child shows a special interest or if you would like more ideas, good references include *Origami in the Classroom* by Chiyo Araki (Tuttle, 1965-68) for the four- to seven-year-old; *Easy Origami* by Dakuohtel Nakano (Puffin, 1994) for the two- to six-year-old; and *The ABCs of Origami* by Claude Sarasas (Tuttle, 1964) for the four- to six-year-old.

PUPPET PLAY

Constructing and playing with puppets improves your child's expressive language and exercises his fine-motor control. Puppetry is an all-encompassing art form. A puppeteer brings an inanimate object to life for an audience. Your child can use his imagination and become another person or thing through the use of puppets.

Materials Needed

Fabric, scissors, paste, yarn, buttons, two paper plates

Activity

Construct finger or hand puppets with felt or other fabric. If you do not have any fabric available, simply use a sock and buttons for eyes and yarn for hair. You may wish to make characters from your child's favorite story. As you read the story, your child can manipulate the puppets.

Variation

Older children would enjoy making paper plate puppets. On a whole plate, have your child draw a face and decorate it. Add yarn for hair, add a hat or earrings, and so on. Cut another paper plate in half. Staple or tape the half plate to the back of the whole plate so that your child's hand fits in between the two plates. He can now make the puppet perform to his delight.

OBSTACLE COURSE

Tasks that involve the limbs and total body will help your child take control of his body. The longer these exercises, the more they build his attention and concentration.

Materials Needed

Household objects such as chairs, tables, boxes, rope, old tires, blankets or towels

Activity

Set up an obstacle course in your backyard using tables and chairs to go under or over, a blanket or towel to roll across boxes to crawl through, old tires to jump in and out of, a rope to jump over, and so on. Encourage your child to move through the course in a variety of ways such as forward, backward, walking, running, or crawling.

BEAN IT

The development of eye-hand coordination is important to many facets of learning. Learning to judge distance, the weight of an object, and speed through space provides practice in coordinating hand and eye movements.

Materials Needed

Posterboard, scissors, beanbags (you can make your own beanbags by sewing two pieces of fabric together around three sides to make a bag. Fill it with beans or rice and then stitch the fourth side closed.)

Activity

Using heavy posterboard, make a target for a beanbag toss. Cut an opening of any shape in the posterboard. For holiday fun, make the hole in the shape of a Halloween pumpkin, a St. Patrick's shamrock, an Easter heart, a Christmas wreath. Choose any holiday symbol you wish. Secure the target so that the beanbag can pass through the opening. Begin by locating the target at close range, increasing the distance as your child's skill improves.

WHO'S ON FIRST?

In addition to training eyes and ears, this activity helps develop pattern recognition.

Materials Needed

Chalk

Activity

One or more children can play this game. On the asphalt or sidewalk, draw several shapes such as squares, circles, rectangles, triangles, octagons, diamonds, and semicircles. Ask each child in turn to perform certain actions such as stand in the shape that has three sides, stand in the shape that has four sides the same length, walk around the shape that has no points, tiptoe around the semicircle. Explain now the names of the shapes to them. Most middle to older children will know which one is the circle, triangle, square, and diamond. After a while they will learn the other names. Keep it fun!

Variation

To make things more complicated, tell each child to stand in a certain shape. With three or more players, have each child start by standing in a designated shape. Then call out, "Circle change with square." As the children become more familiar with the game, just call out two shapes, such as "triangle, square." Those players should quickly change places. For several children, you can make the game more exciting by calling out four shapes at a time, making sure that nobody moves until all four shapes are called.

LET'S PRETEND

Children must learn to isolate the movements of certain muscles and body parts. To write, for instance, they must learn to use the arm and not the whole body. To see something in another part of the room means turning the head, not the entire body. This activity will help children to become aware of body scheme and muscle sense.

 Materials Needed

None

 Activity

Ask your child to pretend his feet are stuck in cement. With his feet very still, give him a series of commands to execute such as reaching as high as possible, bending backward as far as possible, touching the floor with your hands, bending your knees, twisting to the right and then to the left, and so on. This is fun to do with several children at once.

 Variation

Now have the children pretend that cement is stuck to their shoes, and they must move with big weights on each foot. They'll have fun walking like monsters!!

STICKY CANDY

This game will encourage children to think—to resolve a predicament, to anticipate an outcome. It will also prove that a lot of fun can be had when you use your imagination.

 Materials Needed

None

 Activity

Ask a group of the children to think of a candy or a food that is sticky. Lead them to say "marshmallows, taffy, bubble gum," and so on. Have one child pretend he's completely covered with marshmallow. Ask another child to pretend he's pulling the marshmallow off of the first child. Soon the other children will want to join in the fun, and everybody is pretending to pull the sticky substance off of the child. When they realize that some of it is on them, they shake and pull only to get more and more sticky.

This is an especially good activity for a timid child who has a difficult time getting involved in group activities. As he observes the others participating in the fun and the giggles and laughter coming from the group, he cannot resist joining in.

POTATO HEADS

This activity improves coordination, self-confidence, concentration, patience, and body awareness.

Materials Needed

Idaho potatoes

Activity

Have your child stand at one end of a room with as many people as wish to play. Each person places a potato on his head. (Idaho potatoes that are long and flat work the best.) At a given signal (clap of hands or whistle), the players walk across the room keeping the potatoes balanced on their heads. If a potato falls off, the player should immediately pick it up, place it back on his head and continue walking toward the finish line. This game is not designed to produce winners and losers, but to develop your child's ability to balance and walk a straight line, maintaining control over his own body.

POTATO-HEAD RACE

This activity provides the same benefits as in the basic Potato-Head game, but the older child might enjoy some competition with his playmates once he has mastered the latter.

 Materials Needed

Idaho potatoes

 Activity

Form your group into two equal teams. With an odd number of players, let someone be referee so all can participate. The first person on each team places a potato on his head. Players must not touch the potato once it is in position. At a signal, the leaders walk or run across the room, touch a wall, and return to their teams. If the potato falls off during the relay, the player must stop, put it back on his head and continue. Back at the starting point, the player gives the potato to the next person in line. The first team to have all players complete the relay wins.

STEP IN TIME

We strongly agree with Dr. Marie Montessori, the world-renowned nineteenth-century educator who extolled the importance of learning to walk and developing leg muscles. The next four activities will help in a fun way to develop your child's leg muscles and his overall body control. Step in Time increases your child's awareness of his body parts and his ability to direct his body upon command. This activity also enhances muscle sense.

Materials Needed

None

Activity

When you go for walks with your child, practice different movements: walking on tiptoes, walking with legs stiff, skipping, hopping on either foot, walking backward or sideways, marching, and so on. Demonstrate each movement first so that your child can associate the words with the actions. When you feel he understands, make it a game. Clap your hands and at the same time say "hop." Your child should then begin to hop. Clap your hands again and say "skip." Your child should immediately switch to skipping. The pace of this game will depend on your child's age and ability. Begin slowly, and then quicken the pace.

ANIMAL WALKS

Working large muscles through physical activities is important to the overall development of your child. This activity also enriches your child's vocabulary and his concept of the animal kingdom.

Materials Needed

Books or magazines with pictures of various animals

Activity

Your child will enjoy imitating different animal walks or movements (cat, giraffe, elephant, horse, kangaroo, frog, and so on). Have him start at one end of the yard like a cat, for example, then call out "elephant." He should switch to an elephant walk. This is fun indoors as well. Whenever you read a story that mentions an animal, have your child pretend to be that animal.

SNAIL'S PACE

The following activity is fun for the child and develops the leg muscles and body control. Tasks that require the child to move his whole body as slowly as possible help him to gain control of his movements and muscles. Asking a child to focus on such an activity for an extended time will help to build his concentration for work in the classroom.

Materials Needed

Chalk or wide masking tape to use on the floor or on the sidewalk outdoors

Activity

Draw as many parallel lines on the sidewalk as there are children to play the game. The lines must all be the same length with a starting point and a finish point. Have each child stand at the starting point on his line and place one foot in front of the other, heel touching toe. Each child must move down the line in that fashion. Whoever finishes last wins! To add interest and more enjoyment to the game, the children can say or sing this verse:

"Slowly, slowly keep on the line,

Slowly, slowly, I'll get there in time.

Snail, snail, slow down your pace,

Slowly, slowly, I'll win the race."

BALANCE BEAM

Walking on a balance beam develops your child's muscles, and teaches him coordination, balance, and timing. He will also become aware of the capabilities of his arms, legs, head, hands, and feet in daily activities.

Materials Needed

Wide masking tape placed on the floor or concrete for the middle-aged child (five to six) or two-by-four or four-by-six-inch boards for the older child (seven to nine)

Activity

Place a length of wide masking tape in a straight line on the floor or sidewalk. Have your child pretend he is walking on a balance beam. Give him a variety of directions to follow: walk forward on the "beam" touching heel to toe, walk backward, sideways, on tiptoe, with a book on his head. Try whatever variation you think your child can manage. Use the tape to form different shapes (triangle, square, rectangle, diamond, and so on) for your child to "trace" with his feet.

THE LITTLE JUGGLER

Juggling develops a child's coordination, concentration, balance, and timing. He learns control over his body parts. In addition to such obvious physical development, your child will become more self-confident and take pride in his achievement as he improves. He will learn that with determination and practice he can excel at something others cannot do. Praise him often for his efforts.

Materials Needed

Balls, beanbags, or other similar objects

Activity

Have your child toss a ball or beanbag from one hand to the other, while watching the object. Then he can progress to two objects and in time to three. If your child shows a definite interest in this activity, check your local library or book store for more information on juggling. Two excellent books are *The Complete Juggler* by Dave Finnigan (Juggle Bug, 1991) and *Juggler* by Caroline Arnold (Clarion Books, 1988). She is a professional juggler who shares her expertise with young children.

THE LITTLE JUGGLER

How many words can you make
from our little juggler's balls?

1. _____

2. _____

3. _____

4. _____

5. _____

6. _____

7. _____

8. _____

9. _____

10. _____

SAUCER BUBBLES

This activity is calming, enjoyable, and fun to do alone or with a group.

Materials Needed

Flat dish, water, dishwashing liquid, straw

Activity

Provide each child with a flat dish. (A bread and butter plate or saucer works best.) Pour a quarter cup of water into the dish and add one, two, or three teaspoons of dishwashing liquid to make a solution. Dawn® works well. Give the children straws and have them blow into the mix. Beautiful bubbles form on the plate. Soon the children become quite creative with their bubbles, learning to form one inside of the other, depending on how they blow. They usually know enough not to suck too hard or they'll end up with mouths full of soapy water, but it wouldn't hurt to caution them a little! The children are quick to admire their own bubbles and compare them to their neighbor's. This is a great socializing activity; it is not too competitive, but the desire to improve their own soap bubble creation spurs them on. While having fun creating these bubble displays, children are learning about shape and reflection, about density and pressure.

TEXAS COWBOY
BUBBLES

The fun of running wildly through open fields or your backyard is reason enough to engage in this activity.

Materials Needed

Pan, dishwashing soap or glycerin, water, yarn or rope (not plastic)

Activity

Cut a length of rope or heavy yarn that is twelve to eighteen inches long. Soak it in a pan with two ounces of glycerin and two cups of water. You can add more water or more soap so as to make a thick solution. After the rope or yarn is saturated, tie the ends together. Run around twirling the yarn like a lariat, and bubbles will emerge from the loop.

TEXAS COWBOY/COWGIRL SONG

Words and Music By
John and Joan Barrett

Oh I'm a Tex-as cow-boy with a great big cow-boy hat, I've got
Oh I'm a Tex-as cow-girl with a great big cow-girl hat, I've got

(RHYTHM OF HORSES HOOFS)

spurs that jing-gle jang-gle and a horse that's not too fat, I've
rings that shine and glit - ter and I've curls be - neath my hat, I've

got my boots and sad-dle and there's food that's in my pack, I'm
got my trus - ty pin - to and my dog, Chip by my side, I'm

all set to go rid - ing don't know when I'm com - ing back.
head - in' for the prai - rie where I'll ride and ride and ride.

(CHORUS ON NEXT PAGE)

TEXAS COWBOY/COWGIRL SONG

CHORUS

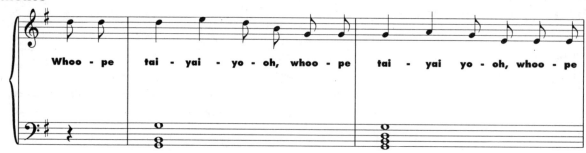

Whoo - pe tai - yai - yo - oh, whoo - pe tai - yai yo - oh, whoo - pe

tai - yai - oh hur - ray - hur - ray, whoo - pe tai - yai yo - oh whoo - pe

tai - yai yo oh, I'm a Tex - as cow - boy, to - day.
(girl)

Now that you enjoy each other's company and can communicate with ease, you might enjoy more extensive activities together. You could go on a nature walk with your child and observe birds and wildlife. Build a birdhouse or make a bird feeder. It doesn't have to be perfect, but the beauty is that it was handmade by the two of you. Praise your child for her efforts. Tell her how proud you are of her and why. Her self-esteem will increase in leaps and bounds with your sincere praise.

On the pages that follow you will find easy bird feeders to make from recycled materials around your home. We've also included a recipe for a wonderful meal for birds—they love it!

BE A BIRD NESTER

Bird study does not require rare birds or wilderness area. Your local birds are ideal for studying since they coexist with people, and children of all ages everywhere enjoy watching them. In addition, your child will develop an appreciation of nature's creatures and an awareness of the need to care about our feathered friends. The following activities teach your child to create and make useful objects from recycled materials.

 ## Materials Needed

Colored yarn or string, thread, small strips of cloth, feathers, hair, twine, small twigs, an empty mesh produce bag, berry containers

 ## Activity

Help a bird build a nest. Cut the yarn and other cloth pieces into three-or-four inch lengths. Fill the mesh bag. Let some of the yarn or thread hang out of the mesh openings to entice the birds to come and take it for nest building. Or, recycle two plastic berry containers. When empty, fill one with the nesting materials. Cover this basket with the other empty basket, both openings together. Attach with string and hang it from a tree.

BE A BIRD FEEDER

Your child will enjoy discovering the countless possibilities of creating a bird feeder from items around the house. We've mentioned a few. The sense of accomplishment in a worthwhile activity as this is beneficial in developing the whole child. Your child will remember forever the experience of sharing and caring for others that he enjoyed learning to do with you.

 ## Materials Needed

See each feeder type

 ## Activity

GOURD FEEDER: Birds love the gourd's seeds and pulp. Purchase a gourd from your local supermarket or fruit and vegetable market. Make a hole the size of a quarter in it and another on the opposite side. Work a twig or branch through the hole and out the opposite side to serve as a perch for the birds. Put a string or wire around the stem and hang it from a tree.

BE A BIRD FEEDER

GRAPEFRUIT, ORANGE, OR COCONUT FEEDERS: Empty grapefruit, or orange halves are easy for you and children of all ages to turn into bird feeders. Insert a piece of wire through the grapefruit or orange half or through the "eyes" of the coconut. Form a hook at one end of the wire with which to hang the feeder and at the other end of the wire tie a knot. Have your child fill the rind or shell half with birdseed. Let her choose where to hang her new feeder.

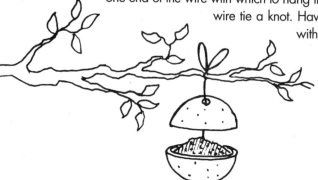

PINECONE FEEDERS: Pinecone feeders are easy for small children to make. Rub peanut butter onto a pinecone. Roll the peanut-buttered cone in bird seed, tie a string to the top end, and hang it outdoors.

MILK CARTON FEEDER A half-gallon plastic or cardboard milk carton makes an excellent feeder. Cut a hole in the side of the carton and fill it with birdseed. Attach a string around the lid and hang it from a tree branch.

BE A BIRD FEEDER

GOBBLEDYGOOK: Make a gourmet meal for your feathered friends using:

   1 pound shortening

   1 cup hot water

   2 cups oatmeal

   4 cups birdseed

   Flour

   Large pan, mixing spoons, and bowl

Soften the shortening over warm heat in a large pan. Add all ingredients with enough flour to make it all stick together. Add other ingredients to suit your fancy—seeds, raisins, grits, and so on.

This is a messy, gooey activity that delights young children. Let them fill the bird feeders or smear Gobbledygook on the branches of an old Christmas tree.

BIG HELPER DINNER

Another fun thing to do together is to actually plan a dinner from beginning to end. All of the recipes that follow use ground beef as the basic ingredient for the main course, and all are easy to prepare.

Materials Needed

See recipes that follow

Activity

Let's plan an international dinner. Perhaps your "Big Helper" has a friend he'd enjoy having over as a guest. Have your child help with setting the table. He can put the placemats around for the number of people attending the dinner. You set one place as an example. Explain as you do it, that the plate goes here, the forks go on the left of the plate, and the knives and spoons on the right. The water glass is placed at the tip of the knife and the salad plate at the tip of the fork. Napkins are placed to the left of the fork. He'll be glad to put the ice in the glasses after you take the ice cubes from the refrigerator and put them in a bowl for him to distribute.

Salad

Your child can help you make a salad. Let him stand on a chair at the sink. You regulate the temperature of the water and let him rinse the vegetables to his heart's content. Even a two-year old can tear lettuce leaves! You can cut up the ingredients and he can put them in a bowl. Add all the ingredients you both agree on.

Main Course

Starting with a pound of ground beef, you can develop an entire meal. A pound of ground beef can serve a traditional all-American favorite—hamburgers. Big Helper will enjoy patting out balls of meat into flat circles and placing them on a cookie sheet for you to broil. When ready to serve, your child can set out the ketchup, mustard, chopped onions and all the fixings to serve with the hamburgers. For another all-American meal, slice English muffins in half horizontally. Place the sliced muffins on a rimmed cookie sheet and pour canned pizza sauce over them. Big Helper can crumble the meat mixture onto the muffins and distribute bits of green pepper, olives, and mushrooms, and onions over the sauce. Top with slices of mozzarella cheese. Pop in the oven for eight to ten minutes or until the cheese is bubbly. Big Helper is now ready to serve his all-American meal.

For an Italian theme, Big Helper can mix the pound of ground beef in a bowl with a raw egg and seasonings you suggest for meatballs. While he squashes the mixture with his

BIG HELPER DINNER

hands and forms it into little balls, you can cook the spaghetti. Fry the meatballs in a tablespoon of oil for five or ten minutes. Serve them in a ready-made sauce over spaghetti or make the "No-Cook Fresh Tomato Sauce" below.

The recipe for the "No-Cook Fresh Tomato Sauce" is:

> 6 large ripe tomatoes (or 18-20 Italian plum tomatoes)
> 4-5 garlic cloves peeled and minced
> Small handful of basil leaves
> 1 teaspoon oregano
> 1/2 cup olive oil
> 1/2 teaspoon salt
> 1/2 teaspoon freshly ground pepper
> 1/2 cup grated parmesan cheese
> 1 pound thin pasta, such as vermicelli or spaghetti

1. Cut each tomato in half crosswise. Squeeze out seeds into the sink. Chop tomatoes into small pieces.

2. Place tomatoes, garlic, basil, oregano, oil, salt, pepper, and cheese in large bowl and mix thoroughly. Leave at room temperature for at least two hours, stirring occasionally.

3. Cook and drain pasta. Pour sauce over pasta. Arrange meatballs around pasta and serve. Pass around more parmesan cheese for your guests to put on their pasta.

Recipe reprinted by permission of The Young Cooks Series, a cooking school for teens 83 E. Elm Street, Chicago, Illinois 60611. (312) 664-1396. Instructors: Robin M. Parsons and Linda A. Bergonia.

For a Polish, Turkish, or Greek theme, make taraba, a popular dish in central and eastern Europe. Brown the meatball mixture in a frying pan with a little butter and ketchup for three minutes. Remove from the heat to cool, roll the meatballs in steamed cabbage leaves, and place them in a casserole. Now add three tablespoons of lemon juice into the frying pan and pour over the cabbage balls in the casserole dish. Cook for $1^1/_2$ hours. Serve on a bed of cooked rice.

Let Big Helper prepare the rice by measuring out two cups of rice to be added to two cups of boiling water and a Tablespoon butter. After boiling for three minutes, the rice should absorb all the water. What a marvelous transformation for your child to observe!

For a Scandinavian theme, use the meatball mixture with the addition of a half teaspoon of celery seed and a quarter teaspoon of nutmeg. Have Big Helper form the balls and place them in a casserole. Add a can of chicken or mushroom soup, cover, and simmer for fifteen or twenty minutes. Serve with rice or noodles.

BIG HELPER DINNER

Dessert

What could be better for dessert than a tray cake? The real surprise is decorating the cake with the flag that represents your heritage. Using a packaged mix or your favorite cake recipe, your Big Helper can mix and bake it.

As the cake cools, prepare the frosting using a store-bought frosting or one prepared with a box of confectioner's sugar. Let your child add food coloring to create a flag. Divide the frosting according to the number of colors on the flag, for instance: Israel and Greece—blue and white; Turkey and Switzerland—red and white; Italy and Hungary—red, white, and green; Ireland—green, white, and orange, of course, America—red, white, and blue. See page 103 for a reference guide to flags of various countries.

Decorations

If you and your Big Helper wish to decorate for your dinner party, you could make paper chains using the country's colors. Cut three-inch strips from appropriately colored paper into circles and glue each one, interlocking them together. The French have a lovely custom of making paper crackers as party favors to be placed at each place setting. Use a ten-by-six-inch sheet of paper. Overlap one-half inch on the two ten-inch edges. Hold the edges together with clear tape. Slip candies, little toys, and trinkets through one end into the middle. Twist crackers three inches in from each end. Now your guest has something to take home.

1) Form a cylinder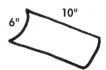
6" 10"

2) Add tape

3) X-ray view of hidden treats

4) Twist crackers

WORLD FLAGS

Canada

Hungary

Spain

Greece

United States

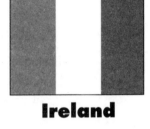

Ireland

Turkey

Germany

France

Italy

Israel

United Kingdom

TOSS A SALAD PUZZLE

Directions:

Lettuce is the main ingredient in our vegetable salad. From the list below, fill in the blanks with the words of the items that are in the salad with the lettuce.

L E T T U C E

Tomatoes, Carrots, Croutons, Radishes, Cucumbers, Celery, Olives

PRESCHOOL

Brown, Margaret Wise. *Goodnight Moon.* New York: HarperCollins, 1947.

Hill, Eric. *Where's Spot?* New York: Puffin, 1994.

Krauss, Ruth. *A Hole Is to Dig.* New York: HarperCollins, 1990.

McCloskey, Robert. *Blueberries for Sal.* New York: Puffin, 1993.

Murphy, Jill. *Five Minutes' Peace.* New York: Putnam, 1989.

Parish, Peggy. *I Can, Can You?* New York: Greenwillow, 1990.

Stevenson, James. *Are We Almost There?* Coral Gables, FL: Shaw, 1992.

PRESCHOOL-KINDERGARTEN

Alexander, Martha. *When the Baby Comes Home, I'm Moving Out.* New York: Dial, 1981.

Fassler, Joan. *Howie Helps Himself.* Morton Grove, IL: Albert Whitman, 1975.

McPhail, David. *Henry Bear's Park.* Boston: Little Brown, 1976.

Rylant, Cynthia. *Henry and Mudge in Puddle Trouble: The Second Book of Their Adventures.* New York: Macmillan, 1987.

Tazewell, Charles. *The Littlest Angel.* Nashville, TN: Hambleton-Hill, 1991.

Vigna, Judith. *Boot Weather.* Morton Grove, IL: Albert Whitman, 1989.

PRESCHOOL-Grade 1

Bang, Molly. *Ten, Nine, Eight.* New York: Greenwillow, 1991.

Kelley, Emily. *Christmas Around the World.* Minneapolis, MN: Carolrhoda, 1986.

Kitamura, Satashi. *When Sheep Cannot Sleep.* Compton, CA: Santillana Publishing, 1986.

Lobel, Arnold. *A Zoo for Mister Muster.* New York: HarperCollins, 1962.

Martin, Bill Jr. *Brown Bear, Brown Bear, What Do You See?* New York: Holt, 1983.

Milford, Sue & Jerry. *Maggie and the Good-bye Gift.* New York: Lothrop, Lee & Shephard, 1979.

Ormerod, Jan. *Moonlight.* New York: Lothrop, Lee & Shepard, 1982.

Waber, Bernard. *But Names Will Never Hurt Me.* Boston: Houghton Mifflin, 1976.

Wells, Rosemary. *Noisy Nora.* New York: Dial, 1973.

Wood, Audrey. *Little Penguin's Tale.* New York: Harcourt Brace Jovanovich, 19??.

PRESCHOOL-Grade 2

Araki, Chiyo. *Origami in the Classroom.* Boston, MA: Tuttle, 1965-68.

Carle, Eric. *The Very Hungry Caterpillar.* New York: Putnam, 1991.

Freeman, Don. *Norman the Doorman.* New York: Viking, 1959.

Graham, Margaret. *Be Nice to Spiders.* New York: HarperCollins 1967.

Hoban, Tana. *Circles, Triangles, and Squares.* New York: Macmillan, 1974.

Waber, Bernard. *Ira Sleeps Over.* Boston: Houghton Mifflin, 1973.

PRESCHOOL-Grade 3

Alexander, Martha. *Move Over Twerp.* New York: Dial, 1989.

Carrick, Carol. *The Foundling.* Boston: Houghton, 1977.

Curtis, Jamie Lee. *When I Was Little: A Four-year-old's Memoir of Her Youth.* New York: HarperCollins, 1993.

Freedman, Florence B. *Brothers: A Hebrew Legend.* New York: HarperCollins, 1985.

Hamm, Diane J. *Grandma Drives a Motor Bed.* Morton Grove, IL: Albert Whitman, 1987.

Lillie, Patricia. *When This Box Is Full.* New York: Greenwillow, 1994.

Ormondroyd, Edward. *Broderick.* Boston: Houghton Mifflin, 1984.

Peters, Sharon. *Animals at Night.* Mahwah, NJ: Troll, 1983.

Pringle, Lawrence. *Octopus Hug.* Hanesdale, PA: Boyds Mill Press, 1993.

Zolotow, Charlotte. *William's Doll.* New York: HarperCollins, 1972.

KINDERGARTEN-Grade 1

Aylesworth, Jim. *My Son John.* New York: Holt, 1994.

Burningham, John. *First Steps.* Cambridge, MA: Candlewick Press, 1994.

Hest, Amy. *Ruby's Storm.* New York: Four Winds Press, 1994.

Howland, Naomi. *ABCDRIVE!* New York: Clarion, 1994.

King, Christopher. *The Vegetables Go To Bed.* New York: Crown, 1994.

Krauss, Ruth. *The Carrot Seed.* New York: HarperCollins, 1986.

McNaughton, Colin. *Making Friends With Frankenstein: A Book of Poems and Pictures.* Cambridge, MA: Candlewick Press, 1994.

Stevens, Janet. *How the Manx Cat Lost Its Tail.* New York: Harcourt Brace Jovanovich, 1990.

KINDERGARTEN-Grade 2

Haas, Irene. *The Maggie B.* New York: Macmillan, 1975.

Heller, Ruth. *The Reason for a Flower.* New York: Putnam, 1983.

Kellogg, Steven. *Can I Keep Him?* New York: Dial, 1971.

Kuskin, Karla. *Something Sleeping in the Hall.* New York: HarperCollins, 1985.

Minarik, Else Holmelund. *A Kiss for Little Bear.* New York: HarperCollins, 1968.

Pinkwater, Daniel Manus. *Big Orange Splot.* Mamaroneck, NY: Hastings House, 1992.

Piper, Watty. *The Little Engine That Could.* New York: Putnam, 1991.

Silverstein, Shel. *The Giving Tree.* New York: HarperCollins, 1964.

Taylor, Mark. *Henry the Explorer.* New York: Little, Brown, 1988.

Viorst, Judith. *The Tenth Good Thing About Barney.* New York: Macmillan, 1971.

Waber, Bernard. *The House on East 88th Street.* Boston: Houghton Mifflin, 1975.

Wilder, Laura. *The Little House on the Prairie.* New York: HarperCollins, 1991.

KINDERGARTEN-Grade 3

Ackerman, Karen. *By The Dawn's Early Light.* New York: Atheneum, 1994.

Ackerman, Karen. *Song and Dance Man.* New York: Knopf, 1988.

Arnold, Katya. *Baba Yaga.* New York: North South Books, 1994.

Barrett, Judi. *Cloudy with a Chance of Meatballs.* New York: Macmillan, 1978.

Girard, Linda W. *Adoption Is for Always.* Morton Grove, IL: Albert Whitman, 1986.

Schwartz, Amy. *Bea & Mr. Jones.* New York: Puffin, 1983.

Williams, Vera B. *Cherries and Cherry Pits.* New York: Greenwillow, 1986.

Grades 1-2

Benchley, Nathaniel. *A Ghost Named Fred.* New York: HarperCollins, 1968.

Greene, Ellen. *Billy Beg and His Bull: An Irish Tale.* New York: Holiday House, YEAR?

Hughes, Shirley. *Moving Molly.* New York: Lothrop Lee & Shephard, 1988.

Kellogg, Steven. *The Mystery of the Stolen Blue Paint.* New York: Dial, 1986.

Kharms, Daniil. *The Story of a Boy Named Will, Who Went Sledding Down the Hill.* New York: North South Books, 1994.

Lamorisse, Art. *The Red Balloon.* New York: Doubleday, 1967.

McCully, Emily. *My Real Family.* San Diego, CA: Harcourt Brace Joranovich, 1994.

Zion, Gene. *Harry the Dirty Dog.* New York: HarperCollins, 1956.

Grades 1-3

Burns, Marilyn. *The Hanukkah Book.* New York: Macmillan, 1981.

Cherry, Lynn. *The Armadillo from Amarillo.* San Diego, CA: Harcourt Brace, 1994.

Greenfield, Eloise. *Me and Nessie.* New York: HarperCollins, 1975.

Johnston, Tony. *The Old Lady and the Birds.* San Diego, CA: Harcourt Brace, 1994.

Most, Bernard. *Whatever Happened to the Dinosaurs?* New York: Harcourt Brace Jovanovich, 1984.

Stevenson, James. *What's Under My Bed?* New York: Greenwillow, 1983.

Waddell, Martin. *Farmer Duck.* Cambridge, MA: Candlewick Press, 1992.

Yolen, Jane. *Letting Swift River Go.* New York: Little Brown, 1992.

Grades 2-3

Barrett, Mary Beth. *Sing to the Stars.* New York: Little Brown, 1994.

Baylor, Byrd. *And It Is Still That Way: Legends Told by Arizona Indian Children.* Santa Fe, NM: Trails West, 1987.

Calmenson, Stephanie. *Marigold and Grandma on the Town.* New York: HarperCollins, 1994.

Ginsburg, Mirra, ed. *The Chinese Mirror.* New York: Harcourt Brace Jovanovich, 1988.

Hughes, Shirley. *An Evening at Alfie's.* New York: Lothrop Lee & Shephard, 1985.

McCully, Emily. *Mariette on High Wire.* New York: Putnam, 1993.

Polacco, Patricia. *Chicken Sunday.* New Yorl: Putnam, 1993.

Grades 2-6

Andersen, Hans Christian. *The Steadfast Tin Soldier.* New York: HarperCollins, 1992.

Arnold, Caroline. *Juggler.* New York: Clarion Books, 1988.

Bancroft, Catherine and Hannah Gruenberg. *Felix's Hat.* New York: Four Winds, 1993.

Boyd, Lizi. *The Not-so-Wicked Stepmother.* New York: Puffin, 1989.

Cassidy, Sylvia and Kunichiro Suelake. *Red Dragonfly on My Shoulder.* New York: HarperCollins, 1992.

Cooney, Barbara. *The Little Juggler.* Mamaroneck, NY: Hastings House, 1982.

dePaola, Tomie. *Tom.* New York: Putnam, 1993.

Finnigan, Dave. *The Complete Juggler.* Edmonds, WA: Jugglebug, 1991.

Joyce, William. *Bently and Egg.* New York: HarperCollins, 1992.

Nakano, Dokuohtei. *Easy Origami.* New York: Viking, 1986.

Williams, Shirley Anne. *Working Cotton.* New Yorl: Harcourt Brace, 1992.

Grades 3-6

Cleary, Beverly. *Ramona and Her Father.* New York: Dell, 1923.

Nordstrom, Ursula. *The Secret Language.* New York: Harper, 1960.

McHugh, Elisabet. *Beethoven's Cat.* New York: Dell, 1991.

Roy, Ron. *Frankie's Staying Back.* Boston: Houghton, 1981.

Sheldon, Dyan. *My Brother is a Visitor From Another Planet.* London: Candlewick, 1993.

Taylor, Sydney. *All-of-a-Kind Family.* New York: Dell, 1980.

White, E.B. *The Trumpet of the Swan.* New York: HarperCollins, 1970.

Wilder, Laura Ingalls. *The Little House on the Prairie.* New York: HarperCollins, 1991.

Grades 4-6

Coatsworth, Elizabeth. *The Cat Who Went to Heaven.* New York: Macmillan, 1967.

Fitzhugh, Louise. *Harriet The Spy.* New York: HarperCollins, 1964.

Fonteyn, Margaret. *Swan Lake.* New York: Harcourt Brace Jovanovich, 1989.

Lenski, Lois. *Strawberry Girl.* New York: Harper, 1945.

Lindberg, Anne. *Travel Far, Pay No Fare.* New York: HarperCollins, 1992.

Sachs, Elizabeth Ann. *Just Like Always.* New York: Macmillan, 1981.

Sarasas, Claude. *The ABCs of Origami: Paper Folding for Children.* Boston: Tuttle, 1964.

Smith, Doris B. *Kelly's Creek.* New York: HarperCollins, 1989.

Wallace, Barbara Brooks. *Peppermints in the Parlor.* New York: Macmillan, 1993.